Beaches of Baja

Beaches of Baja

Revised Edition

by
Walt Wheelock

La Siesta Press

1972

related La Siesta publications:

L. Burr Belden
BAJA CALIFORNIA OVERLAND

Helen Ellsberg
LOS CORONADOS ISLANDS

David Goldbaum
TOWNS OF BAJA CALIFORNIA

Randall Henderson
PALM CANYONS OF BAJA CALIFORNIA

Tina Kasbeer
FLORA OF BAJA NORTE

John W. Robinson
CAMPING AND CLIMBING IN BAJA

Walt Wheelock
BYROADS OF BAJA

LA SIESTA PRESS
Box 406
Glendale, California, 91209
PRINTED IN U. S. A.

SBN-910856-28-1

Contents

ALL PHOTOS NOT OTHERWISE CREDITED ARE BY AUTHOR

Foreword

TIJUANA proudly claims the title of 'The Most Visited City of the World'. Last year, Yosemite, the most visited of our National Parks was panicked with an influx of two million visitors. Tijuana graciously entertained twenty million. With the completion of the tollway to Ensenada, many more are continuing south to enjoy the charm of a city that is not just a border town. Still, while Tijuana is proudly proclaiming its growth as an industrial and cultural center, the vast majority of Norteamericanos never get past the 'tourist traps' of Avenue Revolución and the race track at Agua Caliente.

But many Southern Californians, starved for beach and water recreation, have discovered Bahía Todos Santos with San Miguel Village, Ensenada and Estero Beach, as well as San Felipe on the shores of the Gulf of California.

Yet from the very northwest corner of the nation at El Monumental with busy Playa de Tijuana to the isolated strand below Punta Baja, near El Rosario, is a continuous line of delightful beaches that may have as many as a half dozen cars on a busy weekend — often they rest in solitude.

Many of these, in fact all that are described in this work, may be reached by careful drivers in most ordinary passenger cars. Pickup trucks, campers and VWs roll over these side roads with no trouble, while 4-wheelers can leave their front hubs unlocked. But remember Baja California roads should be driven the way that Bajacalifornios drive. Follow a native driver, who drives a car that you and I would hesitate to take beyond a phone call to the friendly auto clubs, and observe his techniques carefully. He drives at three to ten miles an hour, because he has learned that the bone-shaking ruts can cause screws to climb out of their sockets. At this speed a retread will stand up, where the high-speed blow of a pointed rock will rupture a top-grade new tire. At times he will hesitate, so much so that you may feel he is taking a siesta. But, no — he is alert and attentive. Ahead is a high rock in the roadway. He will decide whether he can swing around it, perhaps straddle it, or maybe it will be better, señor, to climb up one side and down the other. This seems the hard way to a driver accustomed only to freeway travel, but our seasoned Baja driver knows that in this way he will continue on, rather than face a long walk out for help.

So with a little care in chosing the best roads, one may enjoy Playa de Tijuana, San Miguel Village, Estero Beach and Punta Banda and never get off the black-top. But if you will drive with just a bit of care, such primitive beaches as Puerto Santo Tomás, San Juan de Las Pulgas and Camalu-by-the-Sea await you. On the Gulf side, Playa Estrella and Puertocitos are within an hour's drive of the pavement.

But may we make one request? These delightful primitive areas are yours to enjoy; please leave them that way for the next journeyer (it might be you again). Tin cans preferably should be packed out; if not, gathered and chucked into the channel of a sandy arroyo where the next flash flood will bury them forever. Nothing is more disgusting than to go to your favorite campsite and find a ring of beer and pop cans, where the previous visitor has sat on his broad seat and tossed each empty can over his shoulder.

Dwellers of the metropolitan regions of Alta California have the feeling that the lands south of the border must be a hot desert area, to be avoided during the summer months. Nothing could be farther from the truth. San Diego boasts it has the most enjoyable climate of all of the United States. The Pacific coastal regions south of the line are even more pleasant. During the winter months, frosts are almost unknown, the days bright and clear, except when a very occasional rain slips down from the north. But even if one is caught in one of these, a couple of days pass; the mud dries, again on its way to dust.

In the late spring and early summer, high fogs roll in, late in the afternoon, to stay with you until mid-morning. This may even last well into the summer. During one August hot-spell, when the temperature in Los Angeles was pushing a 100°, we found the weather at San Juan de Las Pulgas was reaching 70° at noon, and dropping to 60° during the pre-dawn hours.

Much of the western coastline is formed from old marine terraces, that are lush with flowers that gather much of their moisture from the air, such as the aguave and the astounding vidrîo (crystal iceplant), that may be so watersoaked as to require care in walking over it.

The Gulf coast tends to be much more desert-like, reaching uncomfortable temperatures during the summer months, a la Imperial Valley. But then, there will be no fogs to bother your sun-bathing.

-8-

La Frontera

JUST thirty years after Columbus landed on the West Indies and a scant three years after Hernán Cortés entered Mexico City a settlement and shipyard was established on the Pacific coast at Zacatula, some 150 miles northwest of the present resort of Acapulco. From Zacatula in 1533 an expedition, finally headed by Fortin Jiménez, crossed the Gulf of California, landing near the present site of La Paz. Here Jiménez and many of his force met death at the hands of the Indians. Two years later, hearing rumors of large quantities of pearls, Cortéz himself led an expedition to this same region in an aborative attempt to found a colony at La Paz.

With a complete record of failure, Baja California was left alone for the next century and a half. What exploring was done was by navigators cruising the shores and the beachs of this long slender peninsula, under orders of the King of Spain.

In 1578, His Majesty's forgotten land was forcibly brought to his attention. Francis Drake (who was to be knighted for his exploits) rounded Cape Horn into the unguarded treasure house of King Philip. As he made his way up the coast, he sacked ports and seized ships, picking up first 800 pounds of silver, then 80 pounds of gold, and at last 'six and twenty ton of silver' when he captured a great Spanish treasure galleon. Drake continued north to near the present Bay of San Francisco, where he careened his ship, took possession of the land for Her Majesty Queen Elizabeth I, then returned to England via the Sandwich Islands. Drake's voyage was well publicised and led other freebooters to attempt similar sorties. This in turn forced His Spanish Majesty to give thought to establishing an outpost at a Baja California port to protect his treasure ships and Manila galleons.

Still, no settlements were attempted again until 1683. The Society of Jesus had sent a young missionary, Eusebio Francisco Kino, to the New World in 1681. Although Kino had hoped to work with the heathen in China, his lot was cast with New Spain, first in Baja California, then in Sonora. This dedicated man, probably one of the most effective administrators of the Jesuits, arrived at La Paz on April 1, 1683. A settlement was started and progress was being made, when after some minor thievery, a cannon was fired into a group of Indians to teach them a lesson. Three were killed, others wounded and the Indians revolted. Panic-stricken, the party fled to the mainland. Kino returned to Pimería Alta to continue his missionary work in that field. Baja California was not to be his.

It fell to Kino's companion Jesuit, Juan María Salvatierra, to found the first successful mission in Baja California. On October 19, 1697, ground was broken for the church of Our Lady of Loreto. While often on the verge of starvation, the padres carried on, expanding south to Cabo San Lucas and north into the Viscaíno Desert. Here, the last of an even score of Jesuit missions was established at Santa Maria, near Bahía San Luis Gonzaga.

The Jesuits had a unique opportunity to establish a theocracy in Baja California. Not only were they the spiritual and civil authority, but even the military took orders from the priests. All attempts at settlement or mining were discouraged, if not absolutely forbidden. La Paz had been noted for its pearls, but the padres attempted to prevent the use of the Indians in pearl fishing. In the meantime their missions in Sonora were becoming wealthy, their administrators more powerful; Kino never hesitating to fight or balk the civil governor of Pimería Alta if he felt the welfare of his missions demanded it. Such actions led first to suspicion, then anxiety, and finally to actual fear of the all-powerful Society of Jesus. In the meantime, intrigues in the court of Carlos III took advantage of this situation and in 1767 the Jesuits were expelled from all of the Spanish dominions including those of Pimería Alta and Baja California.

In 1768 the Franciscan order replaced the Jesuits, and the following year moved to the frontier, where they established their first mission at San Fernando Velicatá, some 45 miles east of El Rosario. Beyond here lay the unexplored new frontier of northern Baja California. But the Franciscans were not to work in this isolated region, that was to bear the name, La Frontera. Even when Alta California was settled, and until the end of the 1890's, the name remained in use.

The Franciscans received orders to immediately occupy the two great ports of Alta California, San Diego and Monterey. Leapfrogging north, missions were founded there in 1769 and in 1770. Apparently the lush valleys of California seduced the Franciscans after their struggles with the arid wastes of the Viscaíno Desert, for they never returned to La Frontera.

Fortunately, for them, an opportunity to leave this region graciously presented itself. The Dominican Order of Preaching

Friars, never as powerful as the Jesuits or the Franciscans, nevertheless had a worthy record in the New World, both in Guatemala and Oaxaca. Upon the expulsion of the Jesuits, they asked that their Order be allowed to share in the harvest of souls in Baja California.

Negotiations went on between the King, the Viceroy, and the Orders, and finally the King commanded the Viceroy to assign them suitable districts and sites, totally separated from and independent of the Franciscans. The Viceroy allowed the two Orders to work out the divisions, and in April, 1772, a 'Concordat' gave the Dominicans the old Jesuit missions of Baja California and the lands north to the present boundary of the Californias. This was more than the Dominicans had bargained for, as the older southern missions had become quite decadent. It seemed that a Baja California mission had a prosperous life of about fifty years. At first baptisms were many times the number of deaths, showing both an influx of converts and a healthy crop of babies. But soon, smallpox epidemics slaughtered off large numbers of the natives, and the slow but steady drain of syphilis killed adults and produced still-born babies. The populations dropped to the point where little was to be had in maintaining the establishments. Such was the status of the older missions on May 12, 1773, when the field was turned over to Fray Vicente Mora of the Dominicans.

Governor Pedro Fages in a report has this to say, "The missions of San José, Santiago, Todos Santos, San Javier, Loreto, Comondú, Cadegoma, Guadalupe and Mulegé are on the way to total extinction. The reason is so evident that it leaves no doubt. Syphilis has taken possession of both sexes to such a degree that mothers do not conceive, and if they do conceive, the fetus is born with little hope of living."

The good fathers just could not realize that the Baja California Indians had over many centuries developed a way of life suited to their own needs. To the padres nudity was identical to sin, and the only proper way of clean living was within the closed, roofed room. The Indians had found that they were most happy in an entirely different format. Men went completely naked, not even bothering with a breechclout. On being questioned, one savage told that if he clothed his member, his women did not like it. The women usually wore a small apron of reeds, but as reeds are brittle, quite often this apron would be reduced to a very few strands before the woman got around to replacing her garment. Many of the Indians felt oppressed if they were forced to sleep where they could not see the stars.

Since the natives had no sense of sanitary engineering, only their habit of living in the briefest of shelters, and frequently moving their place of residence, insured a relatively clean living space. When they were forced to return each night to the same room, these would become unspeakably filthy.

Likewise, their social mores were shocking to the fathers. With frequent wars, there was usually a surplus of women. There is no place for an unattached woman in this type of culture, so polygamy was widespread. As if this was not bad enough, the pitahaya harvest festivals completely overwhelmed the padres. Due to the barrenness of the land, the Indians lived in small social groups called rancherías (in recent times this word has come to mean an Indian place of residence – originally it meant the resident group). These rancherías were usually in a state of 'cold war' with their neighbors, so that there would be no chance for social contacts outside of their own little clan. Such a closure would lead to acute inbreeding with all of its evils. The only time of the year when food was plentiful or even abundant was the time of the pitahaya harvest. Then tribal feuds were laid aside and all joined in a 'fandango' that lasted as long as the crop. This was a time of good will and love – and to the padres' horror, this universal love-making was not only general but quite specific – thus providing the women with genes outside their own small group, to the vast improvement of the race. The fathers, as soon as they had the gentiles under control, locked them up at night, the single men in one room, the unmarried women and girls in another, and only those that they considered properly married were allowed to live together. It is almost certain that the priests' idea of what constituted a proper marriage was not what their subjects had been accustomed to practicing.

It would appear that the Franciscans had originally planned on just handing over these decadent missions to the Dominicans. It was only when the Dominicans insisted on having the virgin territory between San Fernando Velicatá and San Diego thrown in, that La Frontera was included. Apparently the departing missionaries felt that this was a cheap price to be shut of the faltering southern missions.

The Dominicans were to establish five 'Pacific missions', two sierra missions, an interior mission, and finally to relocate the northmost of the Pacific missions. The five major missions were all located near the coastal plain, not too far from the shoreline, but none were at the beachs. The Spanish padres disliked cold weather, and the cool damp coastal fogs of much of the year weren't of their liking. The first mission, El Rosario, just east of the little town of that name, was established by Mora, probably in July of 1774. After thirty years, the site was moved south of the arroyo, about a mile from the village, and some five miles from the beach. El Rosario was the largest of the missions; it having an estimated population of just over a thousand souls; yet by 1849 this had dropped to 25.

On about the first of September of the following year, the second of the Pacific missions was founded at Santo Domingo, named for the patron saint of the Order. Located at the mouth of Santo Domingo Cañon, it was later moved two miles up the canyon to a better watered location. This mission served the broad San Quintin plain, with its excellent harbor and profitable salt works. The sea otter provided an additional source of income. The mission was about twenty miles from the harbor, but until the drilling of deep wells, this was the last dependable water source. The Indian population of the region was large; there is evidence of three healthy rancherías in the area – still the mission growth was slow. While El Rosario showed 565 baptisms the first year, Santo Domingo had but two and only three the next (of these, two ran away and were never returned). The peak figure, that of 1800, was 315 souls, and the population had fallen to twenty five by 1849.

Five years went by before the third mission was founded at San Vicente Ferrer. From the date of its establishment in 1780 until 1849, San Vicente was the capital of La Frontera. Here the military commander resided. although his entire 'army', distributed throughout the vast area usually amounted to but two or three dozen soldiers, with perhaps ten at the 'capital'. Often only two or three would be stationed at a mission, which tells of the docility of the coastal Baja Indians. (The Hopis or Apaches would have easily handled this problem on the first dark night.) San Vicente's largest population figure was 317 Indians in 1787. By 1849 there were seven, and in 1853 the listing was 'some Indians, as well as 15 other residents'.

Expansion reached a standstill, until the King commanded that some new missions be established to protect the road to Alta California. Accordingly, on March 28, 1787, the Mission of San Miguel Arcangel (also known as San Miguel de la Frontera) was founded about ten miles east of the present village of La Misión, 37 miles south of the border. Later it was moved to a site at La Misión, where the adobe ruins may be seen just back of a schoolhouse. This is the closest to the beach of any of the missions, being only a mile from the estero at the canyon mouth. Fish and shell fish were important foods of the local Indians, as the large middens indicate. Also south of the mouth of the canyon, about three miles, is La Salina, an important salt works. San Miguel got off to a good start, and reached a maximum population of 400 in 1824. However a severe washout destroyed much of the farm lands and after this the emphasis was placed on the new mission at Descanso.

In 1791, Mission Santo Tomás was founded in an extensive valley some 30 miles south of Ensenada. The first site chosen was down the arroyo about four miles from the present highway. Contrary to the usual problem, this mission was moved, not because of the lack of water, but because the marshy lands nearby were considered unhealthy. Three springs were found near the present location of the village, and the mission reestablished there, three years later. Santo Tomás flourished from the start, raising crops, fruits and grapes, and maintaining extensive herds and flocks. Not only that, but the harbor at the mouth of the arroyo was the only one commonly used between San Quintín and Ensenada. The mission attained a population of 262 in 1800, and was reported to have had 400 in 1824. When the capital was moved from San Vicente in 1849 to Santo Tomás, the population of the village was given at 60, and the mission had the only padre that the Dominicans retained in La Frontera.

Feeling that the vast interior of the frontier should also enjoy the blessing of Christianity, two sierra missions were next established, San Pedro Mártir (1794-1806) and Santa Catalina (1797-1840). These missions led a troubled life. San Pedro Mártir had a much cooler climate, being about a mile high, giving it a climate of about the same severity as the Willamette Valley of Oregon. But a climate that attracted New England settlers was deemed too rugged by the Spaniards. Santa Catalina was lower (3500 feet). Both were primarily used to raise cattle, though a little grain was raised at Santa Catalina.

The Dominicans previously had been fortunate in settling among docile Indians and had little trouble. However, it seems that mountain-living breeds independence, and they were never able to 'reduce' these tribes. Continued attacks made life in the missions too dangerous. San Pedro Mártir was abandoned about 1806, and Santa Catalina was sacked and burned in 1840.

The mission at Descanso was first established as an assisteria of San Miguel, then when that missions fields were washed away, Descanso took over. It is believed to have taken on mission status in 1814 and was abandoned in 1834.

A final mission was started in a broad inland valley east of San Miguel in 1834. Known as Guadalupe del Norte, it had an excellent location, good fields and ample grazing lands. There were a number of rancherías to supply converts. However,

-14-

these natives of the mountains didn't take too well to reduction. Jatñil, a powerful Indian chief at Nejí, was friendly at first and helpful toward the padres, but when enforced baptism and enslavement became a general practice, Jatñil became enraged and led a rebellion in 1840. Father Caballero fled for his life, not even stopping to gather up his cattle. Guadalupe's time as a mission was over. A Russian settlement was established in 1905, and in recent years an extensive agriculture colony has taken over the lands.

The principles of the Revolution of 1821 were not compatible with the mission system, and but two Dominican padres remained in La Frontera. By 1839 there was but one priest left, and he left in 1849. As Meigs* points out, "Whatever else the missions may have handed down, they left an area which was nearly cleared of Indians and made ready for unopposed occupation by settlers." So a steady flow of immigrants from the mainland and from Alta California made their way into La Frontera. The flow from the mainland was accelerated by the discovery of gold in 1848.

Two other factors changed the course of events in the latter part of the nineteenth century; first, the discovery of placer gold deposits at Real del Castillo, Socorro and El Alamo during this period. From 1871 to 1882 Real del Castillo was the seat of the government of La Frontera. The capital was then moved to Ensenada, and finally to Mexicali in 1915. The second factor was a large scale American land project, the International Company, which received leases to much of La Frontera in 1884. They planned extensive developments at Ensenada, San Quintín and Punta Banda. Their plans for dry farming fell after a series of arid years. Fortunately for them, a couple of wet years allowed them to unload on a British syndicate near the end of 1888. The new company constructed a flour mill at San Quintín and started a railway from there to Ensenada. This company was practically bankrupt by 1892 and work on the railroad ceased. By 1906 there was very little activity, but the company's concessions were revalidated that year. In 1917, President Carranza decreed the contract null and void.

At about the same time the Mexican government assumed an active interest in agricultural development. Agarian colonies were established and several irrigation dams constructed. In later years deep wells have been driven into the broad coastal plains and other projects, known as ejidos, have been started. While many of these villages have the raw look of a frontier town, the total increase in agricultural activity has been enormous and bids fair to continue.

*The Dominican Mission Frontier of Lower California.

About 1920 marked the beginning of tourism in Baja California. With prohibition in the United States, and the establishment of legal gambling and other sordid entertainments, Tijuana took on a tarnished glamour that is still remembered by many residents of California. After the repeal of prohibition in the United States, the closing of gambling, and the control of other more questionable activities, Baja California moved into a new era of tourist activities. Good motels, clean restaurants, simplified border regulations – all have encouraged Norte Americanos to vacation below the border. The recent advent of car campers and vans, coupled with a continuing improvement of the back roads have resulted in a happy combination of opportunities to visit the lesser known parts of La Frontera. Some of the most attractive spots are the little known, isolated Baja Beachs.

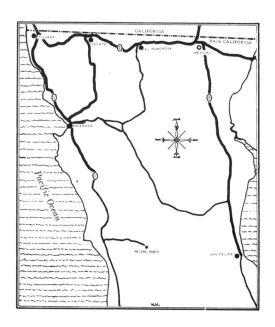

The Everchanging Roads

For years ine roads and roadways never seem to change. Perhaps the ruts on the dirt roads are a little deeper and pits on the blacktop can be depended on to suddenly appear. The many alternate detours in the more remote areas continue to attempt to find better routes around the mud holes.

Then came the toll road and these tolls provided funds to repair and rebuild the old roads. Finally after twenty-five years, it appears that the new blacktop is about to enter Vallé de San Quintín.

Specifically, here some of the recent changes:

For years Mex 1 was measured from Tijuana and the road posts bore those numbers. Then in 1971 the way south from Ensenada was marked from the center of that city, so the new numbers are 104 less. The Puerto Santo Tomás turnoff is now K37 instead of K151, K181 is now K77, etc.

The narrow bridges along the highway used to be fearsome places when you met a truck or bus. Then in 1970 these were marked as one-way. But these often were even more dangerous as many tourists did not understand the change. Now all of the bridges are being widened, but are very rough during the transition.

A new scenic multi-lane highway is being constructed to bypass Calle Primera in Ensenada. It is open as far as the Hotel Santa Isabel and a contract has been let to finish it.

The highway below Ensenada is being widened to Maneadero and by the spring of 1972 was over half finished. A bridge at the south end of Ensenada across the Arroyo del Gallo has meant a dusty detour for sixteen months. Remember this when somebody tells you the entire Baja road will be paved by the end of 1972, or 1973, or any immediate date.

The new road is now entering Colonia Guerrero and should reach Valle de San Quintín some time in 1973. Local papers brag of the speed of paving — a kilometer or a mile a day — but never mention it may take two or three weeks to prepare the roadbed for this sudden burst of speedy pavement.

So we can only say that Baja roads never change and are always changing, and may it always be so.

1972

El Monumental

On a small bluff, just above the sandy Playas de Tijuana stands a slender marble spire that marks the northwestern corner of Mexico, the western end of the peaceful frontier between Baja and Alta California.

But, in spite of the peacefulness, there is no legal crossing here, so one must really return to the border stations at Tijuana to begin his trip to the Beaches of Baja.

The first sight is of a magnificently wide sweeping arch that straddles a dozen lanes of traffic. This is a combination of a welcoming arch, a pedestrian overpass, and an office building for governmental agencies. By comparison, the U.S. border facilities appear most drab. After a quick stop to ascertain if the car is carrying commercial quantities of goods, the visitor is waved on — for Ciudad de Tijuana is justifiably proud of its title: 'The Most Visited City of the World'. And this is no idle boast. The USNPS is worried because of the influx of two million visitors last year at Yosemite, our heaviest visited national park. Tijuana welcomes twenty million visitors each year, and takes it all in stride.

With the opening of the new toll road, the traffic situation has been overhauled. Now the traffic signals have bright lights, rather than the 25w bulbs of yesteryear. Clean clear new signs tell the way through the city, and excellent clear directional markers indicate the routes in the country.

Just south of the gate, at the first signal, the two routes divide. The old route, Camino Libre, signed 'Mex 1', continues straight ahead to Blvd. Reforma, then left to a center monument, and finally right on Ave. Benito Juárez. Leaving the city, it climbs up a small canyon to a mesa, passing La Joya (the jewel) and other small shopping centers, before dropping to the coastal plain, near Rosarito, where it intersects the new highway. Since the completion of the toll road, this free road is being worked over and is now in the best shape it has been for years.

At the border intersection, the new route, signed 'Mex 1D' [directo] turns sharply to the right. As the road crosses Río

SHIPWRECK SOUTH OF SALSIPUEDES
PHOTO BY TINA KASBEER

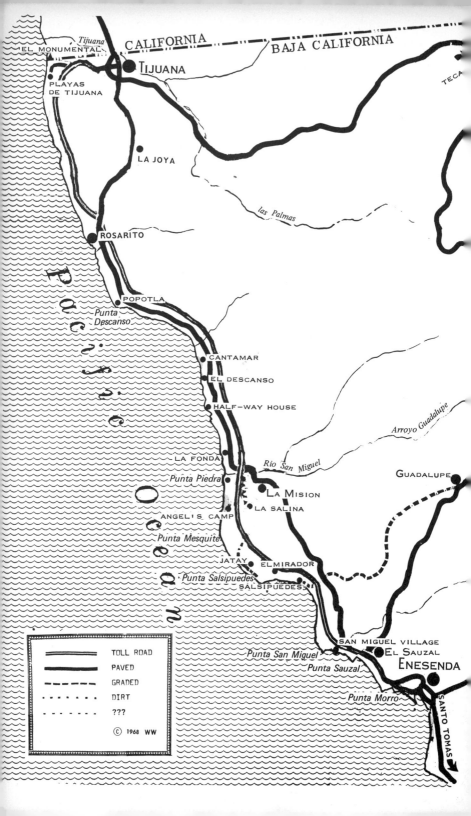

Tijuana, it splits, the south-bound traffic crossing on a bridge, the north via a ford (except in times of heavy rains). Rió Tijuana runs northwest and empties into the Pacific well north in San Diego Co. The United States and Mexico are undertaking a joint multi-million dollar project to eliminate flood damage.

Entering Tijuana on Ave. Revolución, the highway turns to the right on Calle Segunda [Second St.] and continues west to the beach area of El Monumental and Playas' de Tijuana. In the city, straight ahead, is the tourist row of Ave. Revolución. Here flamboyant neon signs call attention to bars, girlie shows, cheap shops, and all the things that might separate a tourist from his dollars. Unfortunately, much of the merchandise, including the shows and the girls are of an inferior grade. A block or two away are found good shops that sell honest merchandise, shops that cater to the many Tijuanese that throng these sidewalks. Still, one is always amazed at prices; because in this border city, the US dollar is the going coinage. Prices are usually marked MA [moneda american], with the other price of MN [moneda nacional] in small type. Shops expect US currency and change is given in the same, even in the smaller shops. A careful and knowledgeable shopper will find worth-while purchases, though not as often as in the earlier days when the tariff 'free list' was more inclusive. The casual shopper may enjoy his thrills, and if it turns out that the little shopkeeper was the smarter, charge it off to education.

The road west on Calle Segunda is lined with large department stores, and it is amazing to see the numbers of zapaterías [shoe stores] — yet on a Saturday or Sunday, they always seem to be doing a thriving trade. Two miles west, by the cemetery, the divided road begins. Passing through heavy cuts and across a steep arroyo, filled with marginal homes, the highway emerges on the coastal plain. Four miles from Ave. Revolución an offramp leads down toward the sea. Looming up on the border, is Plaza El Monumental, reported to be the second largest bullring in all of Mexico.

North of the bull-ring is a chainlink fence leading to the edge of a thirty foot bluff. Here is a tall white marble spire, Monument No. 1, of the long line of border markers stretching from the Pacific to the Gulf of Mexico. The marble was supposed to be ever enduring — to stand for all time, but souvenir hunters soon began chipping of mementos and it was found necessary to surround it with a six-foot high barb-wire topped fence to protect it. The fence (which incidentally often has a narrow passageway through it at the Monument) continues down to the shoreline. But no wire fence could put up with the bat-

tering of the ocean waves, so near the sands, there are a few forlorn looking fence posts, as the fence gives up any attempt of continuing to the broad Pacific. In a like manner, on a warm Sunday, pairs of Tijuanese who wish to be alone, carry blankets a few hundred feet beyond. If there is an Immigration Officer posted on the bluff, he seems to feel that the tide of fun lovers likewise do not need to be held too closely to the International Line, a far cry from the Iron Curtains across the waters.

Along the highway, real estate signs (Lotes, etc.) clutter the scenery, and it seems certain that Playas de Tijuana is experiencing a boom. Newspaper ads urge parents to move to the beach, so as to raise their niños in the clean pure air away from the city — something that startles one used to the really high grade polution of Los Angeles.

The shore line road continues past ever-increasing fraccions [subdivisions] to Costa Azul [blue coast] and ends at La Vigia [the lookout], two miles below the border.

From El Monumental offramp, the expressway continues south. Near is the first Caseta de Cobra [toll house], where a charge of 60¢ is made. There seems to be a bit of confusion as to the method of collecting tolls. Americans seem to think that a fee is charged for a specific stretch of road. But, contrary to the Norteamericano way of building toll roads, these roads have numerous off and on ramps. One may enter a section of road, ride for a while, then leave without paying a fee. In this case, one has been riding on the expressway for about three miles without paying a charge. So, tolls are collected at three points, El Monumental, Rosarito, and San Miguel Pt. In the end, it figures out to be about the same, but in a country where in some sections, the toll road is the only highway, a different system was mandatory.

The toll houses are well built and lighted, seem to have almost as many lanes as the San Francisco Bay Bridge, of which only one or two may be open. But they easily handle all of the traffic. Nearby is a rest station, clean and modern, and safe drinking water. Incidentally, near here is seen the first of the International Road Signs, signs that carry no lettering, just a simple self-explanatory picture. So, in a coy fashion, a dripping faucet means a restroom. Look for more, it's fun to dope them out.

From this coastal road on a clear day, Islas Los Coronados, a five mile long group of four islands, seem to be just offshore. Actually, they are seven miles from the nearest land and ten miles from Playas de Tijuana.

The shore line along much of the west coast of Baja California consists of low bluffs, usually thirty or forty feet above the sea. At times this shore terrace may rise to a height of several hundred feet, as at Cabo Colnett. Where there is large inland drainage, at the mouth of arroyos, etc., plains of great extent may be built up. The first encountered is that of Rosarito; the most extensive in La Frontera is that of Valle de San Quintín. At these locations, the shore approach is gentle, even at times blocked by drifting sand dunes. But along much of the coast, the ocean is bordered by a thirty to forty foot marine terrace. Below lies a beach — a beach which may be sandy, rocky or a shingle (pebble) covered strand, depending on what cliff is breaking down to form the surface. However, little arroyos, only a few feet wide, make their way to the shore. Sometimes, they are gentle, usually easy, but at times they may be narrow and steep. Seldom does one have to wander more than a quarter of a mile up or down the coast to find a passage to the beaches. In more populated regions — and here this means where there are a couple of fish shacks — primitive trails lead to the sands.

There are four offramps in this region, La Joya, Punta Bandera, San Antonio and Rancho del Mar. From some of these, access roads lead to the mesas or the shore, at others at the present there seems to be nothing beyond the end of the ramp, a situation that surely will not long endure.

Twelve miles below the El Monumental toll gate, the two highways cross, west to Rosarito, east branch for Mex 1 D.

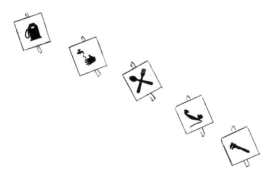

Rosarito Beach

As one approaches the littoral of El Rosarito [little rose] the most impressive sight is that of the large thermoelectric complex near the shore. The neat power plant and the huge oil storage tanks form a landmark, visible for miles at sea. The spidery high-line towers march east, across the Sierra Juárez to the Rió Colorado delta at Mexicali. But even greater developments are in order. Plans call for a nuclear-electric plant that will generate even larger amounts of power, as well as desalted fresh water, so needed in La Frontera.

Next is the offramp at Rosarito Norte. If you take the by-road here, watch your speed — the drop from the toll road speed is easily overlooked — but the speed limit is 30 mph, well posted, and there is usually a patrol car checking.

Rosarito has been steadily growing and has many local shops as well as a number designed to provide for the tourist's fancy. Accommodations range from a free camping beach to the plush Rosarito Beach Hotel, complete with its bars, dining room and orchestra. Other motels provide adequate services.

In the thirties, Rosarito Beach received quite a bit of notoriety, being the scene of the last 'filibuster invasion'. Gambling was declared illegal in Baja California, except for the race track and Jai Alia games. A group of 'big operators' from the Chicago area took a lease on the hotel property and announced that they would open up games. The federales politely informed them that it was illegal; only to be brusquely told that the gang was accustomed to controlling police action, and they certainly did not intend to be annoyed by small-town cops. The casino opened; drew good crowds, then on a weekend, the federales moved in. Away to jail went not only the operators but all of the guests at the gaming tables. Included were a couple of navy lieutenants, who were as loud as the mobsters with their "You Can't Do This To Me" cries. The federales were not impressed by either. A couple of days later saw all the guests safely back across the line, but Casino del Rosarito was finished. After the wave of newspaper publicity, Americans were not about to take a chance here, and there are still those who remember the story and are a little uneasy around the hotel. The

'filibusters' retreated to Cicero and Las Vegas, still trying to figure out what went wrong.

At the south end of El Rosarito is a complex offramp system, which forces local northbound traffic up onto and off the expressway. Nearby is the second toll gate (80¢, please). The toll road cruises toward Ensenada at a higher level, reaching an elevation of 250 feet near the Half Way House. The old road winds closer to the beach, passing a number of small resorts, some of which date back many years; some are ultra-modern. First comes Playa Encantada and the Italian Village, the latter a café that has served tourists for quite some time. Then comes the deluxe trailer court of Popotla [a region in Costa Rico, from which comes the Rodriguez family]. Still in the process of expansion, it offers a large swimming pool, private beach, and trailer hookups. During the summer season, it may be completely filled.

Next we find Mar Azul, El Miramar, Santa Maria, and Raul's at the Cantiles [steep rocks] offramp. In between are many primitive campsites on the bluffs. Some are unattended and no charge is made; at others a charge is made, up to $1.00. Many of the more established ones are upgrading their facilities, and offer better accommodations at somewhat higher rates, though none approach Popotla or Cantamar. Numbers of beach homes are being built, which in time may crowd out the campers. Raul's is a drive-in type of restaurant, clean and good, but closes rather early at night. Just south of here is the very old way-stop of Puerto Nuevo-Newport (both names are displayed). With the building of newer stops, it has faded, but it is hoped that it may again regain its trade. Then comes the thriving hotel and trailer court of Cantamar [singing sea], with an excellent restaurant, orchestra, entertainment, etc. It has been going long enough, so there is a covering of trees and flowers to enhance its beauty.

Three miles beyond Cantamar the toll road crosses a side road to the old mission site of Descanso [no offramp here]. The road follows up an arroyo to an open area, where a small white church has been erected on the mission site. Here was founded the Misîon Descanso [relief] in 1814. There is some question as to whether this was a new mission. A flood had wiped out the crop lands at San Miguel. Descanso had been an out-ranch of San Miguel, and the padre simply moved up the road. Many old documents make little distinction and often documents read 'Misîon Viejo' and 'Misîon Nuevo'. A few buildings including a cantina now stand at the road junction.

South of here, off shore, stands birdlime-whitened Sugar Loaf Rock, while on shore is a blow-hole that operates at high tide.

Near here a road sign reads 'Médanos' [sand dunes]; again no offramp. Huge steep sand dunes rear up alongside of the old road, and on weekends, children and dune buggies run up and slide down the soft slopes. At the north end is a quaint little cantina that sells beer, sodas and 'carnitas'. The latter is a form of roast pork that is sliced and served on tortillas, the Mexican equivalent of a hot dog. And you can be quite sure the meat is fresh, as often the carcass is hanging from the rafters.

At the south end of the dunes there is again a terrace, with many unimproved camp sites. Two miles below is Medio Camino [Half Way House], a resort that dates back to the days when it was a stage stop and the only resting place between Descanso and San Miguel Mision. Unlike most such places, it has kept up with the changing times and is still a good stopping spot. Meals, drinks and cabins are available, and out on the south end, somewhat improved campsites are available for a small fee.

The toll road climbs higher to pass a shoulder of the hills, reaching a height of about 250 feet, to offer a view of the sea. Finally comes the offramp of Alisitos [alder grove], where the roads split, and the old road heads inland for Río San Miguel and the Arroyo Guadalupe, and then climbs up to the mesa to cross over on the way to Ensenada.

Near the turnoff is La Fonda [the inn], a picturesque restaurant perched on the bluff. It is a well-known spot, and before the newer Cantamar and Popotla were built, was the most deluxe stop between Rosarito and Ensenada. If you wish, you may be served on an open-air patio, overlooking the long stretch of sandy shores, but the afternoon breezes may soon drive you in. Below here is one of the best stretches of sandy beaches, and camping is available. To the south is a beach colony, El Mision, with a number of well built private cottages.

High on the hill stands a tall slender cylinder. This is the standpipe for the Tijuana aqueduct. Water is pumped from the wells down beside Río San Miguel, then flows north to the border city.

Salsipuedes

At K51, the expressway (Mex 1D) and the old road (Mex 1) divide. El Camino Libre cuts inland toward Rio San Miguel (Arroyo Guadalupe). The river is crossed on a long bridge,and just at the south end, a dirt road heads west to the beach. The old dirt road along the coast is met after two miles. Crossing Mex 1D through an underpass brings one to Rancho Punta Piedra [rocky point]. Here is a group of vacation homes on the ranch of Jorge Rafael. This area, Punta Piedra, was formerly much used for camping, being easily reached from La Misión bridge. Now Señor Rafael discourages camping, saying it costs more to clean up the tourists' litter than he receives in fees. However, it does present interesting black basaltic rocks for fishing, tide pools, and an excellent sandy beach.

There is no connection with the expressway here, but a dirt road runs along the east side of the right-of-way for two miles to the La Salina offramp and crosses to Angel's Camp and its wide sandy strand.

Driving south from the bridge on Mex 1, one soon reaches La Misión, the site of old Misión San Miguel de la Frontera. Built here in 1782, it replaced an earlier site some seven miles inland. Just behind a small church are a few well-marked adobe ruins, all that remains of the extensive mission.

Climbing upward, the roadway is carved from steep basaltic cliffs as it mounts to the mesa. Numerous grey-white stonecrops (hen-and-chickens) dot these black cliff faces, providing a spectacular effect. Once on top of the mesa, the road cruises along until it enters a narrow canyon, Arroyo de la Carmen, which it follows to the junction with the expressway at San Miguel Village, just south of the last toll house. The old road route is 21.5 miles between junctions.

Following the new expressway, one drops to the estero [lagoon] at the mouth of Rio San Miguel. Four and a half miles below the Alisitos offramp (La Fonda) is La Salina. At the Y below this offramp, the left fork crosses under the road and back to a rancho located near a large white salt sink, the La Salina [saltworks] of mission days. The padres of San Miguel sold salt to passing ships and whalers. The right fork, signed

'La Playa', swings over a sandy road to Angel's Camp (do not wander off the tracks). Here is a wide sandy beach, a cafe, and cabin sites for lease. It is experiencing quite a building boom. The little point here is sometimes called Salsipuedes, but the name more properly belongs to the prominent point two miles southward.

The next offramp is that of Jatay [*Ind*: place of water]. To the east is Rancho Jatay, a stop on the road of the old days. The primitive road can be seen climbing over the hills to the mesa. To the west, the road forks at once. The right branch goes around a little hill, passes a couple of small farm houses and joins a coastal road after a mile and a quarter. A right hand turn takes one to a nearby sandy beach, the left fork has a bad pitch and should be avoided.

Back at the Y, a well traveled road crosses the mesa to the left, then drops to an elevated terrace. This road is not steep, but has a couple of nasty pitches with outcropping rocks. Careful drivers will have no trouble, others may rip a pan. From the terrace, another grade leads down to the marine terrace and a mile of isolated shoreline. Two and a half miles from the highway is the gate of Rancho Los Madrigales. North of the gate is free camping.

A fee of $1.00 is charged for camping on the ranch property, but the area is cleaner, and there are a number of somewhat sheltered campsites. Well water may be obtained at the ranch. The road wanders south along a level bench to a clump of rocks a mile and a half beyond the gate. Here is the true Punta Salsipuedes [get-out-if-you-can]. On the rocky tip, bathed by the ocean's spray is a hand-wrought iron cross, dedicated to the souls of those who 'did not get out'. A short walk away is a protected sandy cove, a good place to bathe.

The basaltic rocks here are an excellent place for rock fishing, and at low tides, mussels and abalones may be taken in season. There is usually a fish camp or two of Mexican shell-fishermen. At times of extreme low tides the camps may swell to several dozen fishermen gathering literally tons of mussels, to be shipped out for food and bait.

Leaving the Jatay offramp, the expressway slowly climbs to an isolated overpass. To the right is a shrine, to the left nothing, in neither case, a connecting road. By climbing under the fence, one may stroll to the top of a knoll, directly above Punta Salsipuedes. But for those who don't wish to spend this energy, here to the south, across the wide expanse of Bahía Salsipuedes, is a view that far excels the famed San Simon of Alta California's Highway 1. Certainly the name of this off-ramp, El Mirador [scenic balcony], was well chosen. Looking ahead, Camino Mexico Uno, can be seen draped across the ridges and terraces for miles, as it winds along side of Bahía Salsipuedes, a five mile long bay that bites almost two miles into the coastline. Off to the south may be seen the Todos Santos Islands and the strong out-thrust of Punta Banda.

Two miles past El Mirador is the Salsipuedes offramp. Here, an old road to the coast crosses Mex 1. Just east of the highway up in a nook of the canyon is a small oasis. Years ago, at this spring, an Englishman lived and planted. Now fruit trees, palms and other domestic plants gone wild, still survive. On the terraces below the road are a number of olive groves and Rancho Salsipuedes. The road down is well graded but steep and should not be attempted in wet weather. Here are more orchards, a reservoir, a rose-covered adobe hacienda, and on the bluff a group of motel units. Trails lead down to the beaches bordering Bahía Salsipuedes.

The next stretch of road is that which held up the opening of the new road for years. Perhaps the sad name of the bahía was a bad omen. The road would be graded, and even blacktopped, and along would come a storm. Floods would wash out the fills — or if the culverts took care of this water, then the unconsolidated fill material would become water-logged and slump. As late as early 1967, a fill just south of here, some 300 yards long and about 100 feet high, gently slipped into the ocean. The engineers, feeling that the native alluvium did not supply satisfactory fill material, trucked thousands of tons of fill from near La Misión. But even yet, minor subsidences occur and sections of the roadway are being rerouted to place them on consolidated soil, rather than on fills. Drive cautiously near here and watch for warning signs.

On the other hand, these cuts and fills provide the only way to get down to the beaches from the highway. Two and a half miles beyond the Salsipuedes offramp, a road-level gravel quarry on the right provides parking space and access to the water line. Shortly beyond, new fish shacks are springing up along the highway, and three miles farther, a draw leads down to the wreck of a ship. Seven miles from Salsipuedes is the San Miguel toll gate ($1.00, por favor).

Bahia Todos Santos

IMMEDIATELY past the last toll-gate, the road crosses Arroyo Carmen, the route of the old Tijuana road. To the right is one of the best coordinated tourist facilities on the peninsula. Here at San Miguel Village, Tomás Robertson provides accommodations ranging from simple beach camping to home-sites for $50,000 residences. In between are trailer pads with hookups, semi-permanent deluxe locations, etc. Señor Robertson's Village has a paved launching ramp with a protecting breakwater and fishing boats may be rented. He is quite an advocate and booster of amiable relations between Norte- and Bajacalifornios.

A couple of miles down the road is the pueblo of El Sauzal, perhaps an older town than Ensenada. It is an active fishing port and cannery site, as well as a cotton processing center. The large pinkish mansion to the right was the home of the late General Abelardo Rodríguez, former governor of both Sonora and Baja California, and president of Mexico. General Rodriguez, recognizing Mexico's acute shortage of edible fats and Baja California's ability to grow olives, pushed the planting of the many orchards and can be said to be the father of this industry.

For those who have not been to Ensenada for some time, this stretch of road will present a surprise. Years ago, the highway followed the shore into the center of the village, then with the building of the breakwater this road was blocked off and all traffic was routed down Avenue 10. Now the new divided highway follows the old coastal route to the port area of Ensenada, but there are no additional toll-houses. An off-ramp still leads to the Avenue 10 route, which is faster for those who might wish to continue south without entering the central business district of the city. Follow Avenue 10 into town, then drop over to Avenue 9 when the ballpark closes this route. Across town this street runs into Avenue Reforma, which is the extension of the main road south. Shortly after leaving Mex 1D on entering the city, a side road right will be found leading up to the summit of Chapultepec Hills, an excellent overlook from which to view and photograph Ensenada.

Ensenada de Todos Santos is the third largest city of Baja California and by far the busiest seaport. For years, after the initial spurt in 1870, it had remained a pleasant small town, and even after the tourism boom struck Tijuana and to a lesser extent Mexicali, Ensenada went its way, being always gracious to those who made their way by the primitive roads from the International Border. During the early prohibition days an attempt was made to cash in on the swarms of norteamericanos who came across the line. A luxury hotel, the Riviera Pacífico was constructed, and it was announced that it was being promoted by Jack Dempsey. However his connections were nominal and failed to strike a spark with the tourists. After several attempts to make a success of the project, it has finally been abandoned.

For years Ensenada accepted, was even friendly toward her USA visitors, but except for a cantina or two, there was little aimed at the tourist. Hussong's Cantina was almost the center of activity. The visitor dropped in there, which looked more like a set from Gunsmoke than a Mexican resort; after a drink (perhaps a cervaza or a margerita), he walked out, bought and tried to find a place to mail a postal card, then headed back for San Diego and points north.

Then came a period of ramshackle expansion, during the '50s and early '60s. Calle Primera sprouted with tourist-souvenir shops, liquor stores and bars interlaced the space, and a half dozen or so 'cabarets' opened. These offered rock-and-roll, Go-Go or 'topless', depending on what Avenue Revolucion in Tijuana was featuring. Avenue Ruíz was lined with more typical Mexican shops offering merchandise for the rancheros who came down from the hills to shop. Hussong's remained unchanged, but now not every tourist stopped in.

Now in the last year or two, Ensenada is brightening up — perhaps the new high-speed highway is bringing a different type of visitor, one who wants chrome and 'native-art' designed spots. The center of tourism has drifted south, still on Calle Primera, but now near Bahía Resort Hotel and El Rey Sol Restaurant. New shops, a modern bookstore, and handicraft spots offer gifts that are in good taste and stress native workmanship. Of course, 'hippies' wander the streets, but look as lost as when they stroll on Sunset Blvd. 'Topless' takes the place of 'strip-teeze' in the tourist traps, but they look a little dusty and lonesome, as though they were a sort of left-over from an era that had marched ahead. Hussong's alone has not been changed. The same rough wood floor, the long bar and the old bar stools are still there. Fifty cents, American, still buys a drink that seems almost too big and good to be true. But the clientel is that of solid Ensenada business men, who drop in for a 'long one' at lunch time. Norteamericanos are seen, but many are those who now live in Ensenada.

If the visitor wishes to see what is going on now in Ensenada de Todos Santos, he should walk down Avenue Juárez (which should be Fifth Avenue). Here is an entirely new part of the city. New, simple buildings line the street, buildings that have been built to serve the people of the city and the surrounding country. The shops carry signs in Spanish, no attempt is made to attract Norteamericano trade. On a Friday or Saturday night, the shops stay open until midnight, the sidewalks filled with countrypeople, who window-shop and drift in and out of the tiendas. — and never a 'hippy'.

Ensenada first started out as a landing place, then grew into the principal port of Baja California. In more recent years, the old rickety long wharf was replaced with a stone breakwater and accompaning piers. These have been steadily improved and expanded, until now Ensenada boasts a well protected harbor and modern loading facilities.

But Bahía Todos Santos has been for years a fisherman's landing, and the new heavy duty facilities have not eliminated the small commercial and sporting fishing. The old hodge-podge collection of fish-stands have been ordered up, but there are still the little spots where one may buy fish directly from the fisherman. The sport-fishing facilities are busier than ever, but there are now large parking lots, and better piers to board the off-shore boats. One may charter boats for $75.00 MA and up, or join with others in a party boat for much less.

With the new awareness of tourism, Ensenada now even has a new floating restaurant, complete with music and all of the other trappings.

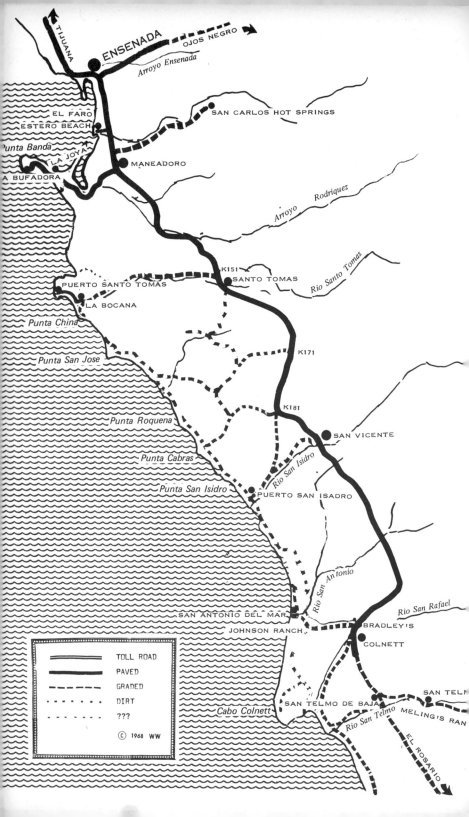

Punta Banda

TEN miles south of Ensenada is the town of Maneadero. This town antedates Ensenada and in mission days was the only inhabitated place on Todos Santos Bay. Now it is a prosperous farming center with a large school, markets and other stores. Mandeadero boasts a population of 4500.

The immigration station that used to be located north of the town has now been moved a mile south of the Punta Banda turnoff. Tourist cards are required below here, but may be obtained at this office with proper proof of U.S. citizenship.

From the south end of the town, a paved road (marked La Bufadora) swings right toward Punta Banda. Heading west, it passes La Grulla Gun Club, which dates from before the turn of the century, and the hacienda of Charles Nordhoff, grandfather of the author of 'Mutiny on the Bounty', who settled here in 1887. Nordhoff, himself, was an author of note, writing several promotional works on the Californias, including one on Baja California. This work, 'Peninsular California', probably the earliest popular publication on La Frontera, contains interesting stories of the times of the International Company, as well as a great deal of misinformation.

Beginning about seven miles west of Mexico 1 is a group of tourist camps, Punta Banda, Agua Caliente, La Joya, etc. The hot springs, Agua Caliente, are famed from the times of the padres, and was to be the site of a 1000-bed hotel and health resort in 1888. Today, a bath house provides two hot showers, quite a come-down from those grandiose plans. But the sight of clouds of steam arising on cold mornings is still a spectacular sight.

Near here, the Punta Banda peninsula pinches together, and provides a low pass across the high ridge. Just beyond La Joya is the Red Store, a small grocery and cafe. Then to the left an unmarked dirt road branches south. The turnoff is masked by a low bluff, but beyond, the road may clearly be seen crawling over the ridge. It may be impassable after a heavy rain. After a half mile the road forks (the second fork, please). The left road climbs up an easy grade over a low spur (450 ft.) and ends in a eucalyptus grove, El Arbolitos, 1.6 miles from the black-

top. This little grove, which shows signs of many years of wood harvesting, provides one of the most picturesque camping spots in the area, somewhat isolated, sheltered, and with an excellent view down a steep gorge, which drops 400 feet to a rocky cove. A primitive trail leads down to a terrace, about forty feet above the sea. Forks lead to the right to a breakdown, and to the left to several others. They are not easy to follow, but if one is careful, he may pick his way almost anywhere through the agave and catsclaw. The second drop to right is said to provide the best fishing. Just offshore, a rocky islet supports a noisy colony of sea-lions. A primitive road climbs left from the grove, across terraces and mesas, with several unmarked forks. Eventually it reaches Maneadero Valley. As it crosses bluffs, trails drop steeply to small coves and a pack trail leads to a small group of farms at Rancho Costia, which may otherwise only be reached by sea. At the mouth of the arroyo at the rancho is a wide sandy beach, the only one on the south side of Punta Banda.

Returning to the fork, a half mile from the blacktop, the right branch leads up a steep rocky road, crosses the ridge at 630 feet, then slides down to a lobster fishery, called Kennedy's Camp – also known as Nuevo Arbolitos. Señor Kennedy, a former American, has lived here for a quarter of a century, back to the time when he had to backpack his lobster catch to Ensenada. Boats may be rented here, rather cheaply, though this is subject to prior negotiation. Of course, there is quite good rockfishing from the black craggy ledges.

Back on the Punta Banda Road, 1.8 miles from La Joya, a side road right drops to a tourist camp, The Three Sisters, three-quarters of a mile from the highway. Camping space and boats may be rented. In the early days, before the breakwater was completed at Ensenada, that anchorage was unprotected against southwest tempests, and ships fled to this region to wait out a storm.

A mile and a half west of the Three Sisters junction, the road crosses to the south side of the ridge. A dirt road leaves the pass and runs right for 0.2 mile to the north, to an overlook of Bahía Todos Santos. This dirt road continues west, but it is badly cut up and ends in a cul-de-sac after a mile. Better hike it — and it is worth it! A quarter of a mile beyond this parking area, a faint trail leads up the ridge to the summit (1273 ft.). However the undergrowth is sparse, and it is easy to pick a route if the trail is missed. From the summit on a clear day, a panorama may be enjoyed from Punta Salsipuedes to

Punta Santo Tomás, over the coast with its coves, inlets and rocky islets, as well as to Sierra Occidental, back of Ensenada. If one follows the road to the end — or drops down to it after climbing the peak – it is found to dead end on the side of the peak. A good trail continues over an easy saddle and drops to a terrace that forms the far western end of Punta Banda.

The paved road winds down to a fish camp (store, cafes, boats, etc.) at La Bufadora, 13 miles from Mexico 1. Two hundred feet beyond the road end, over a well marked trail, is a famed blow-hole, La Bufadora [the roarer]. Waves rushing into a crevasse, traps and compresses quantities of air, and on the rebound, water is thrown into the air with a terrific roar. At times, spray reaches a hundred feet up the rocky face. When the sun is right, La Bufadora wears a miniature rainbow to grace her plumes.

Punta Banda peninsula is composed of sedimentary rock, and while beaches are few, there are many rocky coves, where the cliff faces drop directly to deep water, to the delight of the rock fishermen. Cabezon, sheephead and perch are common and easily hooked. This region has repeatedly submerged and then arose again from beneath the sea, forming numerous terraces. Some thirteen may be counted, giving the name of 'Banded Point'.

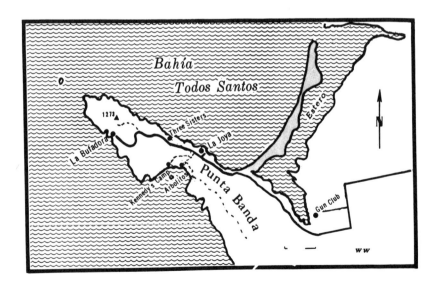

Puerto Santo Tomás

FROM Maneadero, the highway crosses a low shoulder into a large valley to continue south. Off to the left was the old mission rancho of La Grulla [the crane], still a farming region. About 14 miles from Maneadero is a pass over the great Soledad ridge and then the road winds down into Santo Tomás Valley. A mile and a half from the summit, just before the valley floor is reached (K151), an excellent graded road heads down the arroyo to the sea. This road leads to the quarry of Cementos California, S.A., the operators of the large cement works near Ensenada, whose belching smoke stack is an all too visible landmark. The company has graded and maintains the road to Punta China [Point of Pebbles]. After crossing the west end of the valley, the arroyo narrows and large oaks provide shady driving. Usually a small stream meanders under the oaks. Three and a half miles from Mex 1, the adobe ruins of Misión Santo Tomás Viejo are standing on the right. Founded in 1791, the coastal fogs were too much for the padres and in 1794 the establishment was shifted inland to the present site of the village. Small ranchos, growing peppers, tomatoes and alfalfa, occupy the more desirable open spots along Río Santo Tomás. Nine miles from the old mission site, just past a cattle guard, a sideroad right takes off for Bahía Soledad (see below).

Three miles more and the road forks, with the cement road to the left, down the stream bed, up onto a terrace with a landing strip, and on to a locked gate at the limestone quarry of Punta China, 16.7 miles from the paved road. This is a very attractive establishment, with a palm-shaded swimming pool, but it is not open to the public. The quarry is located on the nose of the point and the limestone is loaded into ships to be taken to Ensenada. Beyond the gate, the road did continue to Punta San José, but it is now washed out and impassable.

From the Y, a rather good dirt road cuts right, hugging the toe of the hills for a mile and a half to a camp spot, La Bocana [the mouth], 16.6 miles from the blacktop. Here a tree-bordered meadow affords pleasant camping (50¢ per car, 1967); a well supplies water and sometimes one may buy soft drinks.

Seaward is a small beach, pebbled above the water line, sandy below. South across the mouth, is a cluster of sand dunes. A sign to the right indicates that the road beyond is private property, but tourists are welcome, especially if they patronize the cantina and fishing facilities at the roadhead. The road follows a marine terrace, with numerous promontories providing good but unimproved campsites. Rather high above the water, these offer excellent views of the sea and of sunsets, but in like fashion, may be a bit breezy. At the road end, (2.8 miles from La Bocana), is a small resort, Vista al Mar. A store sells meals, drinks, gas, and a goodly supply of groceries. Cabins are available, as well as fishing boats and guide service. Rock fishing may be enjoyed within a stone throw of the cantina.

Here, at Puerto Santo Tomás was the seaport of the mission, one of the very few sheltered harbors on the west coast of Baja California. The cliffs drop to the water line, and the small coastal boats of colonial days were able to closely approach the shore. By contrast, the sandy beaches of Ensenada were shallow and ships were forced to anchor far offshore.

The sea coast and inland cliffs are composed of limestone, pock-marked with many small caves. The area has only been little explored, and who knows, maybe a large cavern may yet be discovered by spelunkers.

Here on the beach of Puerto Santo Tomás is a typical example of Baja California's famous marine 'upwelling'. The normal current flow is from north to south. As the current sweeps past a point, a large circular whirl is developed. This slow whirlpool pumps the cool waters from beneath the surface, and the water south of many of Baja's points may be as much as ten degrees colder than the waters on the northern shores, a few miles away. Here at the beach below Punta Santo Tomás, one may check out this theory if he cares to try the cold waters.

North lies lonely Bahía Soledad, possibly the least known large bay of La Frontera. The primitive beauty of its wide clean beach is accented by the foaming line of rocks forming Punta Santo Tomás to the south. From the Port, a little used trail climbs to the ridge in a little less than a mile. Here one gazes north to Punta Banda and south to Cabo Colnett. The trail crosses an elevated level terrace and drops to this quiet cove. There are a few fisherman's shacks, which may or not be occupied. Allow three hours for the hike; more for bathing, exploring, fishing, or just simple enjoyment.

From the road junction, 12.5 miles west of the blacktop, a dirt road heads north up a shallow arroyo. Rather good at first, the sharp pitches and tight turns of the u per part calls for a short-coupled 4-wheeler. Better hike over the last shoulder, for not only is it steep and sandy, but the road surface has a tendency to slide off into the canyon at the touchy spots.

Returning to Mex 1, one again heads south. Just across the highway is Rancho de Los Dolores, a large and well cared-for vineyard that for years has supplied grapes for the famed Vinos de Santo Tomás. Now the winery is located at Ensenada and many of the grapes come from Tecate and San Valentín. But Santo Tomás with its morning fogs and brilliant mid-day sun, as well as its limestone-based soils, reminds one of the famed Alta California wine regions of Saratoga.

Two miles, across the valley floor is Santo Tomás, site of the mission of the same name. It seems almost impossible that this little village was once the capital of all of La Frontera. Yet in July, 1849, it became the capital and held this position for twenty-five years, until Real del Castillo took over during the gold strike of the '70s. In this same year of 1849, Father Agustín Mansilla y Gamboa closed his church doors, and the mission period of Baja California ended with the departure of this last of the Dominican friars.

The padres chose Santo Tomás as the second site for the mission because of the warm clear weather and the existence of three large flowing springs. Today, the village is built a-round these same springs. At the entrance to the settlement is a large tourist complex, El Palomar, consisting of a store, cafe, trailer park and swimming pool. Definitely geared to the tourist trade, the prices are not those expected of a small interior village. Beyond here is the native village, with small tiendas, cantinas, a school and a cluster of adobe homes.

West of Santo Tomás, a steep road climbs up the western hills to El Chocolate, now an uninhabited barley rancho, then down the arroyo past small cattle spreads to Rancho San José. Some maps show a road continuing to the sea coast at Punta San Juan, but a mile or so past the rancho is a washout that blocks farther travel. From the appearance of the road surface it would seem that nobody has attempted the trip for a number of years — except on horseback.

Puntas San José y San Isídro

ALONG the coast west of Santo Tomás and San Vicente lies a coastal mesa or terrace that extends from Punta San José to below Punta San Isidro. Almost untouched by tourists and completely ignorant of tourism, it offers pleasant camping. Fishermen or farmers (especially small farm boys) may wander into your fire circle, to pass the time of day, if you have a bit of Spanish, or just sit and communicate without words, as men have always been able to do by the glow of a campfire.

Roads that reach the terrace are in fair shape, but do have sandy stretches and perhaps a steep pitch. Ten miles from Santo Tomás, near K 171, a dirt road crosses the arroyo, and climbs steeply to the ridge, but from here to the coast it is all down hill, with a little light sand as it emerges on the coastal terrace. There are large new grain sheds 5.5 miles from Mex 1, which are indicated on maps as El Refugio. Now the hands live in town, and the land looks like a mid-west wheat baron's spread. The road continues west, following an arroyo that has some water, green truck gardens and small ranchos.

The grain-covered terrace ·is reached at 15.6 miles. The right fork runs north for about five miles, passing a vegetable growing colony, and a couple of cattle ranchos. The bluff lies high above the beach, but arroyos break through to the shore.

On Punta San José is an abandoned fish camp, and around a bend the road heads up a cañon and swings back on the mesa. But on the downhill side, erosion has about wiped it out. It used to continue to Punta China, but is now closed at the quarry.

South, the road runs along the upper edge of the grain fields for 2.5 miles to Rancho San Juan de Las Pulgas [St. John of The Fleas], headquarters for this grain operation. A small arroyo is crossed on a little dam, and at another half mile take the beach fork (left fork is a jeep road over the mesa). The shoreline has bird rocks, basaltic stacks and platforms and a small protected campsite, about 1.2 miles from the ranch. Just to the south of the roadend is an intimate smooth beach, but the rocks on either side throw up tremendous plumes of spray. (Here is just about our favorite Baja campsite). A trail leads around a small point to Bahía Almejas [Clam Beach], where

one can look past a towering black cliff to the road from Puerto San Isidro and Punta Cabras.

Six miles down the main road is a better known junction, K 181. Almost immediately the side road forks; the right one climbing steeply to a mesa, then continuing west. It crosses an area of grain fields and after four miles, a sign 'Punta Cabra Beach' points down canyon. The road picks up a small stream which it follows until you reach a gate at a very small but neat farm at the bottom. Usually a young girl will run out to open the gate for you and will be pleased with a few pieces of candy or a peso. The road turns up canyon, passing a couple of shady campsites, then crosses a mesa, and meets the coastal road just north of Punta Cabra Camp.

The main fork from the highway follows down an arroyo for 7.2 miles to reach Rio San Isidro and the direct road from San Vicente. Just below the junction, note the small closed-cone pines coming almost to the road. These relics from the Ice-Age are the most southerly of coastal pines.

Three miles brings one to Ejido Eréndira and then to Puerto San Isidro. Here is a small tienda where one may buy sodas. There are a few cabins at the port, some of which may be for rent. A fish camp is found after three miles, and a half mile farther the road crests at Punta Cabra [Goat Point]. There is a three-way junction here: left dead-ends in sand dunes, right is the alternate approach from Mex 1, and the center road goes north to a large 'Half Moon Bay'. Here is an excellent smooth beach with lots of camping room, but frigid waters. The road continues over a shoulder, past two fishing camps and a shipwreck to dead end at Punta Roquena [Rocky Point]. Ahead is Bahía Almaje, which we last saw from south of Rancho San Juan de Las Pulgas.

From the Ejido, a road leads south over a basaltic pavement ledge, loaded with blow-holes, for six miles to a camping spot located on a miniature estero. The route cuts inland here, for 13 steep rough miles of isolated road to reach San Antonio del Mar (heavy-duty pickups or 4-wheelers here).

An alternate road leads up Rio San Isidro directly to San Vicente, but has a half-dozen stream crossings, some of which may be quite deep.

SHIPWRECK SOUTH OF PUNTA ROQUENA
PHOTO BY HOWARD GULICK

San Antonio del Mar

BELOW San Vicente, Mex 1 swings through rolling hills, covered with grain fields. Seven miles south of San Vicente the landscape opens up into a wide valley known as Llano Colorado (one of many so-named). Here is one of the most attractive developments along the road. Long rows of tomatoes and chiles cover the flats, while the slopes are set out to olives. On the right, a farmer is raising multi-colored zinnias.

Eleven miles more brings one to the best-known landmark on the Transpeninsular Highway, the infamous 'End-of-the-Pavement'. But like everywhere else, progress comes, and in the summer of 1968, the blacktop started south, after a twenty year pause. Work progresses, but it seems unlikely that it will reach the terminal point, K 300 (just south of the San Quintín turnoff) by the project date of December 1968.

At a point 23 miles south of San Vicente is a service station -cafe named Arroyo Grande, but called by all travelers 'Bradleys'. Nearby is a hospital, staffed by the Flying Samaritans, a group of southern California doctors who own their own planes and fly in to provide good-neighbor medical services.

In the arroyo, a half mile farther along is Colonia Colnett, once a settlement of a few homes, but now grown to be a fair sized community. However the shops and businesses are definitely oriented toward local trade.

From either point, roads lead west, joining near an air strip, to continue on down into the valley of Rio San Antonio. In the olden days, Camino Real ran west of the present road, and here was one of the best known stopping spots on the route, Johnson's Ranch. Harry Johnson raised grain here, had a large cattle spread in the Sierra San Pedro Martír (now known as Meling's Ranch, and operated by his daughter Alberta Johnson Meling and her husband Salvador), and developed the Socorro Gold Mine, once one of the best producers in Baja California.

Two miles farther west are the sand dunes of San Antonio del Mar. This has been a favorite camping spot, with flat sheltered areas protected by the dunes, while over the crest are miles of clean sandy beaches. Two native resorts are located here. On the north is the camp of Florencio Arana, with white-painted buildings, some of which are for rent, and at times his wife will serve meals. South of the flat is the camp of Tony Martinez, who provides open camping spots, sodas, and some food. However he is only open on weekends, etc.

The beach at San Antonio provides some of the best Pismo clamming found anywhere in Baja California. Dune buggies race over the sweeping dunes or follow the low-tide beaches. Here, the south-flowing currents cast up all sorts of flotsam and jetsam, some coming from as far away as Japan, though now, plastic trash seems to be replacing the once famous Jap glass fishfloats. Timbers, even parts of wrecked ships may be found along the beach in the aftermath of a passing storm. The waters are rather mixed-up, so look out for rip tides when currents run strong. Fortunately the waters are quite warm.

However, with the coming of the new highway 'modern progress' has struck San Antonio. A Tijuana-based operation, San Antonio del Mar Club, has taken over the Johnson Ranch and much of the valley floor. They have elaborate plans, including subdividing much of the area, building a large motel, and hope to dredge the estero to form a small boat marina and build an off-shore pier. Camping is still permitted, for a small fee. Florencio and Tony own their lands and plan on still carrying on at the old stands.

Two side trips may be taken. At an isolated hill 0.3 mile from the road end, turn north across the valley floor, then up a short steep hill to the mesa. Another 1.2 miles brings one to a junction. West leads a short distance to the terrace edge, then drops to a bench at the beach. Excellent fishing and a sandy beach may be reached by scrambling north. Isolated.

If one continues on the first road, a Y is reached and the left fork drops to a bench at an arroyo mouth. Spectacular rocks, with several sea arches and a fine beach. CAUTION! do not crawl through the arches on a rising tide — be sure the tide is still going out if you decide to enjoy these hidden spots.

Near Johnson's Ranch, a dirt road leads south into one of the most isolated regions of La Frontera, Cabo Colnett. Road directions are difficult, just head in a southwest direction, and if you meet anyone, ask for 'El Camino a El Faro?' for the tip is marked with a small lighthouse. The road continues to a small parking spot, then plunges down an arroyo. Park and walk, as the track is steep and tortuous. The black cliffs of the Cape loom above you. Ahead is an unbroken stretch of sea, often shrouded with wisps of grey fog, and a feeling of being cut off from the world you know will descend upon you —

Bahía San Quintín

FROM Colnett, two roads are available. By following down Arroyo Colnett (better route along the south side), for about seven miles, one reaches an unimproved coastal road. Across the mouth of the valley is a high gravel berm extending almost to the cliffs on the north. Behind this, a rather sandy road winds two miles to a small fishing village sheltered under the towering cliffs of Cabo Colnett. The Bahía de Colnett provides kelp fishing, butter clams, and commercial lobster fishing. However the 'upwelling' is quite severe here, so the waters are rather chilly. Norteamericanos have driven here for some excellent surfing, but it is only for those who can put up with the arctic waters.

At the south-side road junction is located 'Ramon's Camp', high on a bluff above the shore. Ramon is quite a character, an elderly short man, who lives alone in an 8 8 foot tidy shack. He advertises "guide service, hunting and fishing — English spoken". Sometimes Ramon has a skiff for offshore fishing, othertimes not. His 'english' is basic, to say the least, but he enjoys conversation, such as it is, and it is quite likely that you will too. He does have one of the cleanest camp areas.

The roadway continues south, along the terrace for three miles to the mouth of Arroyo San Telmo. Here is another spot where the south-bound ocean current deposits some of its loot. Perhaps you will be able to pick up Japanese fish floats or other goodies. From the south edge of the arroyo, a single lane, unimproved road follows up the arroyo, always through acres of grain fields, until Mex 1 is joined after 5.5 miles. While this is a primitive road, it is one of the smoothest and fastest, south of the blacktop.

The coast road heads directly south, at times along the coast, or swings inland across the wide coastal terrace. At six miles is the wide spread of Rancho San Francisquito (Sr. Tomás Lacey). This huge operation raises barley and other grains, shipping the better crops, and using the poorer for a large hog raising project. Five miles farther, after rounding Punta San Jacinto, one comes suddenly upon Leo Moreno's Camalu-by-the-Sea. (see below).

The main road from Colonia Colnett crosses Arroyo Colnett and climbs a slight grade before heading south. The road crosses rolling fields, bearing rich crops of grain. Eight miles from Colnett, a wide graded road branches to the east, leading to San Telmo, an ancient mission outpost, then climbs into the Sierra de San Pedro Martir, reaching Rancho San José (Meling Ranch), some 30 miles. Here is a beautiful mountain guest ranch with excellent facilities.*

A mile farther south on the main road is the small village of San Telmo Abajo. An excellent primitive road leads west to the beach, a distance of 5.5 miles (see above).

Three and a half miles brings one to Ejido Ruben Jaramillo. This is a quite extensive agricultural settlement, that seems to have suddenly grown from nowhere, so much so that it is only shown on a single map and is not mentioned in any of the guides to this region. While it is estimated to have a population in excess of 1000, it seems to have but a single cantina and one small store. Incidentally, the red loam here, which also gives this plain its old name of Llano Colorado, can be exceptionally mean during a rainy spell.

Yet this same rich red soil is producing one of the most productive regions of Baja California. Here, and at Valles Camalu and San Quintin, barley and wheat are raised in large quantities. The agriculturists of this area have succeeded in developing a hard wheat, the first to grow in warm climates. Crop specialists have come from as far away as India to investigate and purchase this unique cereal seed. In addition, potatoes, tomatoes and chiles are raised in this frost-free land. Large stands of olive trees grow on the more inland spots. When the surfaced road reaches San Quintin, so that the crops may be more easily marketed, these valleys should experience a fantastic boom. As it is, these combined valleys shipped more than $25,000,000, M.N. of products in 1967.

Below Llano Colorado, the road climbs up an easy ridge, then drops into Valle Camalu. This is another prosperous location that has escaped guide book notice. Older than Ejido Ruben Jaramillo, it has several cafes, cantinas and stores, as well as a large Pemex distributing station. Just at the bottom of the grade, 19 miles south of Colnett, and just to the right of the Pemex station, a good road leads two miles to the sea, at a bright new fisherman's camp, Camalu-by-the-Sea. This is operated by Leo Moreno, who is a most interesting character in his own right. Retiring from the Mexican Army as a sergeant at the age of 55, he decided to settle down. Marrying a 16-year Ensenada orphan, and with a total capital of a few burros, he came here to start a resort. Twelve years later he has six niños, a large substantial home, a couple of fishing boats, four motel units, and is planning on further expansion. Leo's energy and vitality belie his age, and he is most willing to expound on the benefits of his spot in the sun, married life, etc.

Leo's camp stands near the edge of a bluff overlooking Bahía San Ramón and its wide beach stretching away to the volcanos of San Quintín and Isla San Martín. Good surf fishing.

San Quintín valley was the location of several early land developments, the last one, organized in 1890, being the Lower California Development Company of London. They subdivided the land into tracts of 30 acres, promising complete security to any farmer who would plant his tract to orchards. A 17-mile long railroad was constructed that never carried any traffic. A flour mill was built on the bay, but wheat crops failed. The contract was cancelled in 1918.

After many years, the government drilled deep wells and started a modern development, Colonia Guerrero. Lagging at first, substantial buildings were constructed in the early '50s, and now Guerrero is the largest settlement south of Ensenada. With the coming of the blacktop, the expansion should approach boom-stage. Below the main village center, a string of shops, churches, cafes, and other small businesses extend south.

Unfortunately, the native soil has no compacting qualities and the road along the floor of the valley is one that calls for four-letter-words. Apparently broad and smooth, then pot holes as big and as deep as a wash tub suddenly appear in front of the driver. Any attempt to make time here can result in flat tires, broken springs, or even the wiping out of a front end.

Fifteen miles below the Colonia's center is a steam-powered canning plant on the right; then a road west to the Bahía San Quintín resorts. The roadway is wide, but a bit sandy and dusty in dry weather, and any amount of mud in wet weather. Here are located two motels, Ernesto's and El Molino. There is a small wharf and boats may be hired or launched. Ruins include the old mill, the relic of a large steam engine and the remains of the railroad causeway, now without its bridge.

Bahía San Quintín is one of the most beautiful bays on the west coast of Baja California. The inner harbor is almost land locked, and the outer harbor is quite protected except for the swells that occur in times of storms. The channel is marked by a line of buoys, but if you don't have a local pilot, a depth gauge will be well worth while.

While the sport fishing is not the same as near La Paz, it is not uncommon to land a 100-pound black sea bass.

El Rosario-Punta Baja

BELOW the Bahía San Quintín turnoff the main road deterio-
rates rapidly. Not only was the fill never properly compacted,
but the light sandy silt of which it was made could never have
been built into a successful road surface. North of here, some
gravel has been hauled to help the surface, and this continues
to a point 1.7 miles south of the San Quintín turnoff. Below here
is one of the most difficult stretches of Mex 1. Much of the
traffic swings east, along an unimproved dirt road (may be deep
mud after a heavy rain, but the puddles can usually be by-
passed). As it reaches the toe of the foothills it turns south,
reaching the small farming community of San Simón after five
miles. The roadside is fairly well built up for the next two
miles, by which time the community has now acquired the name
of Santa María. At this point, a fair road leads west one mile
to Mex 1, then one may continue south a half mile to the entrance to Santa Maria Sky Ranch, missing the worst stretch of
the 'main highway'. The bypass continues across fields, never
good, but never bad, until it reaches Mex 1, after a distance of
7.2 miles from the point where you had left the 'main highway'.
However, if you wish to use the main highway, saving a mile
or two, at the expense of time and some very rough road, continue south. Soon the road bed collapses, and much of the traffic takes to the ditches. Three miles below the bypass point
(five below the San Quintín junction) the roadway has been completely abandoned. Flowers and shrubs grow on isolated table-
like segments of Mex 1, which has not felt a wheel for some
time. After a little over a mile of this, the roadway will carry
some traffic, but most of the knowledgeable drivers remain in
the ditch roads. Six miles from the San Quintín junction is the
well-marked turnoff to Sky Ranch, a well kept resort, offering
rooms, meals and gasoline, as well as a landing strip (here
is the last aviation gas in La Frontera), and camping facilities.
Just west of the resort is an excellent private beach, where
Pismo clams may be gathered at low tides. The beach is hard-
packed and cars race up and down for miles — but beware of
incoming tides that may cut you off!

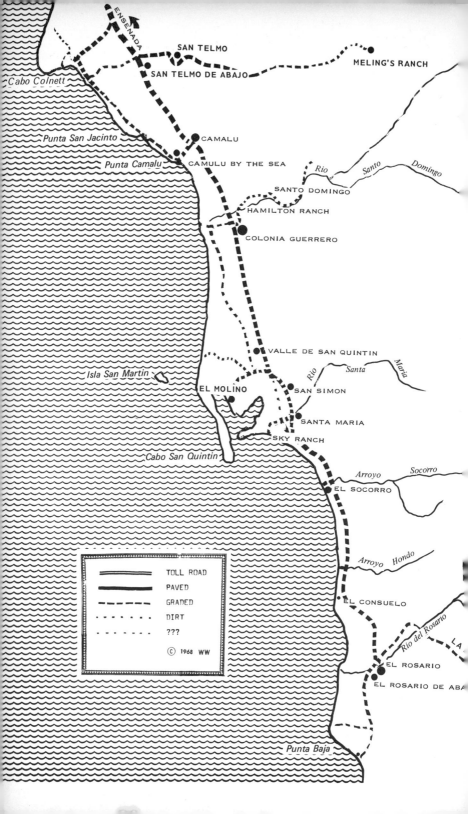

Below the Sky Ranch junction, the road bed is in fair shape, but the surface is still exceptionally rough. Two miles below, is the junction point of Pabellon, where the bypass road enters. A road leads west, 1.6 miles to Pabellon (Pavillion) Beach.

The main road continues south across the usually uninteresting San Quintin Plain. However, in late spring, the iceplant that covers this area puts on a spectacular floral display. It is covered with delicate cream-colored flowers, but the leaves of the plant change from their usual pale green to a rusty-pink, and as it does, the entire plain is a solid sheet of golden-rose. Soon, the display fades, and remains a burnt-out carpet until the following spring.

Three miles below the junction, the constructed roadbed narrows, and it climbs up and across the edge of the foothills on a cobblestone-topped surface. Another two miles, and it returns to the terrace, having successfully avoided a bad area of sand-dunes. If you have the equipment to drive over such, or care to try it on foot, these sand-dunes provide a pleasant, somewhat isolated camping region. But from the main road, three side-roads lead down to the shore line. Signs indicate Rancho Socorro and Rancho Socorrito. If you see a group of olive-drab pyramid tents, this is a summer training area for the Mexican Army reservists. Socorro is a favorite camping spot for Norteamericanos, and several cabins have been built here. It is quite possible that with better roads this will become quite a resort area.

South of here the road construction takes an interesting turn. Across much of this stretch a roadway of two (or more) car width was built. When an arroyo crossing was encountered, it was filled with soil and gravel, hoping that the porous soil would take care of water drainage. Unfortunately, while rainfall is slight, individual storms may be heavy. So cuts were washed through each fill. Now the motorist has two choices. A very steep deep dip may be crossed by going straight ahead. Or a bypass may be found to one side, crawling down an ungraded trail into the arroyo, then winding back up the other side. It will be noted that most local trucking takes the side routes.

Side roads lead off to the terrace edge and primitive camp-sites will be found at the end of these. One can scramble down cuts to the beach, or often work along an arroyo. Seven miles below El Socorro one encounters Arroyo Hondo (also known locally as Arroyo Amargo), where the fill was never completed. A few rocks across the roadway mark this crossing. Observe them! for the road takes a fifty-foot leap into space. A variety

of routes lead off the west side and down onto the arroyo floor. Surprisingly, they are not bad, and may usually be climbed, even after a rain storm.

A side road leads 0.2 mile to a clean (please keep it that way) camping area, one of the most delightful along this roadway. Just to the north of the arroyo mouth are outcroppings of a peculiar grey-green dense sandstone, known as the Rosario Formation. It is a very uniform type of sandstone, completely without fossils or vegetable matter. The wave-action has sculptured it into smooth free-forms that are interesting to study and photograph. A quarter of a mile north, it forms rocky points, from which one may cast for perch or even small leopard sharks.

Two miles south of Arroyo Hondo is the small cafe of El Consuelo, neat and clean and friendly. Señor Collins, who operates this cafe, is a descendant of one of a group of six young Englishmen who deserted a whaler at Cabo San Lucas around 1825. Legend has it that they were a group of English students who had been shanghaied. They all married local señoritas and have produced honored Baja California families.

A mile and a quarter from El Consuelo (inquire from Señor Collins) is a kelp camp located on a sandy terrace overlying a continuous layer of Rosario sandstone, which forms a natural Malecón (boardwalk) just above the high-tide line, and makes excellent fishing platforms. The workers at the camp harvest kelp, which when dried brings 3000 pesos per ton in Ensenada. From here it is shipped to Japan to be processed for agar.

The main road turns inland up an easy grade — a little sandy - to the top of a mesa, some seven miles from El Consuelo. Here to the right is the airport of El Rosario. Just before one reaches the landing strip, a sharp left hand turn leads down into a steep arroyo (low gear, though it is not as bad as it looks at first). Two miles of this brings one to the bottom of the arroyo and another half mile of easy grade, then here is El Rosario.

Slightly east of the present Pueblo of El Rosario, are the remains of the first of the Dominican missions, founded in 1774. Later, after one of the still recurring floods, the mission was moved across the arroyo and downstream to the present site of El Rosario de Abajo. After the missions were secularized the first land grant was made to Carlos Espinosa. Ever since that time the Espinosas have lived in this region. Señora Anita Espinosa now operates a cafe, provides rooms and has one of the two gas pumps in town. (Warning: the next gas pump is

330 miles away at San Ignacio, though gas may be obtained at way points – siphoned from barrels.)

Señora Espinosa is known as the Angel of Baja. She is ever ready to provide information, arrange for assistance in times of disaster, and keeps a motherly check on Norteamericanos who venture into the isolated reaches beyond, to ascertain when they return to this last outpost of civilization.

Two roads lead to the beaches from here. The more direct runs down the north bank of the arroyo, swinging around now and then, where a planted field has pre-empted the roadway, until the mouth of Rio Rosario is reached at 4.7 miles. Usually there is a large fresh-water estero located here, but the disastrous flood of September 1967 washed out the protecting sand-bar. It is slowly recovering, and without a repeat of the storm, should again be a favorite fishing spot in a couple more years.

But as old as El Rosario is, there are signs of much earlier life. On the hills to the north of the arroyo are located 'digs', where paleontologists are studying deposits of dinosaur bones.

At the west edge of the pueblo, the road forks, the left branch heading across the arroyo to El Rosario de Abajo (the streambed crossing is the dustiest and the sandiest stretch that you will find on this road). A mile and a half brings you to this step-child of El Rosario. Tarry awhile, because here are located ruins of the second mission church, as well as a number of large homes and commercial buildings that date from the later Colonial Period. Now a number of small modern homes are being built, but the business center of the region is north of the arroyo.

A single track, but surprizingly good road swings south, climbing up a long arroyo. Near the top (6 miles from the village), a fork leads right 2.5 miles to Punta Baja. The left road works across a couple of arroyos to finally reach the coastal terrace. At 10.3 miles from the center of El Rosario is another road fork. The right one leads down, in a half mile, to a large abalone camp. Here, located on the shores of Bahía del Rosario, is one of the most fantastically beautiful of the beaches of Baja. Miles of gentle sandy strand extend in both directions, sheltered by the extension of Punta Baja. Offshore looms Isla San Geronimo, an isolated barren rock, nine miles southward from Punta Baja and five miles offshore. Here is a place to spend hours, days or weeks.

Sea of Cortez

INSTEAD of following the Pacific coastline south, one may cross the peninsula to Mexicali and enjoy the beaches of the Sea of Cortez. A good highway (Mex 2) leads out Blvd. Agua Caliente, past the racetrack, and climbs gentle grades for thirty miles to the city of Tecate. Here is a most unusual community, a city located on the border that definitely is not a 'border town'. Certainly tourists are welcome and accomodations are good and modern, but Tecate is a young brisk city that depends on its own industries for its living and growth. Here is the Tecate Brewery that makes the famous beer of that name. But also located here is the largest malt works in all of Mexico, and much of the barley that is raised on the coastal terraces comes here, to be shipped out as malt, to be used by breweries located throughout the entire nation.

Just east and south of here are extensive vineyards, and many of the grapes are shipped to Ensenada to reappear as Santo Tomás Wines. Eastward, Mex 2 winds over gentle rolling country to crest after 40 miles at La Rumorosa. An enjoyable side trip along a fair dirt road may be made to the south along the crest through piñon and pine forests for some 48 miles to the shores of Laguna Hanson, by far the largest mountain lake in Baja California.*

East from La Rumorosa, Mex 2 drops swiftly down the spectacular Cantu Grade to the dry lake of Laguna Salada, then on over a low pass to Mexicali, the capital of the State of Baja California. It is a total of 117 miles from Tijuana, all on an highway. However, if one wishes, he may drive directly to Mexicali from the Los Angeles area, via the Salton Sea route, saving about thirty miles, at the expense of many miles of delightful seashore and mountain touring.

The Mexicali Valley, on the delta of Rio Colorado, would be expected to supply many beaches, but actually there are almost none. Located at about sea-level, with miles of land that may be deep in sand or slime, neither the river banks or the Gulf shores are easily reached. By crossing the river at San Luis, one may continue south to El Golfo de Santa Clara, the

* Camping and Climbing in Baja

nearest resort on the Sea of Cortez from Los Angeles, but after all, this is in Sonora, not Baja California.

From Mexicali, Highway Mex 5 heads south toward San Felipe. This is a good black-topped highway, that runs along the eastern toe of the Sierra Cucapás. In years gone by, before the Rio Colorado was tamed and hog-tied by a series of dams, the river lashed back and forth with each spring torrent, form- ing a number of alternate channels. The fartherest west, and one of the most stable of its routes, was the Rio Hardy.

Forty miles south of Mexicali are two fishing camps, El Mayor and Campo Rio Hardy. While these can hardly be called 'beaches', there are landing places, with boats, fishing sup- plies, trailer camps, modest stores, etc., the only convenient spot in Baja California, where one can reach a branch of the Rio Colorado. The highway continues south around the end of the Sierra Cucupás, and several wheel-tracks cross the salt flats, by means of which one may possibly reach the main channel of the Colorado. But probably it would be better to try this with a 4-wheel-drive rig, and a careful choosing of the right time of the year.

The highway continues south, past the sand dunes of La Ventana and a vast uninhabited region, until about a 115 miles below Mexicali, one finds the first of the group of fish-trailer camps that give access to the Gulf of California. Here are La Ramando, El Paraiso, Playa las Amejas, and perhaps, by the time you arrive, one or two more camping spots. These offer various degrees of accommodations: camping sites, launching ramps, possibly a cafe of sorts, but certainly soft drinks and cerveza.

Finally, a 125 miles from Mexicali, after crossing a slight rise, the fishing village of San Felipe appears, on the blue Sea of Cortez. While San Felipe is mentioned in accounts dating back to the time of the Jesuits, when Padre Linck led an ex- pedition overland from the south, and later when Mountain Man James Ohio Pattie crossed near here on a westward trapping expedition, it only became a place of permanant residence around 1948 when Gov. Rodríguez promoted an auto highway.

San Felipe now provides good motels, adequate fishing facil- ities, several unpretentious shops and modest cantinas. The high tides make the beaches exciting and an occasional chubasco such as that of September 1967, provides an element of exciting adventure to this gulf port. The totuava fishing here once drew many fishermen to try this sport, but unfortunately, not con- tent with sport fishing, the commercial fishermen overfished

NATIVE QUARTERS, SAN FELIPE

the region, and it will be some time before the totuava schools will completely recover.

This vast inland sea has some thousand miles of shoreline off the Baja California coast and even more on the mainland. With north-bound currents, it is probably the largest fish trap in all of the world. But not only are fish trapped in this long, ever-narrowing slot, but the tide waters themselves are likewise being crowded and squeezed, so that the tide crest rises higher and higher as it approaches the northern limit. Tides at La Paz run some 4.5 feet. By the time that Bahía de Los Angeles has been reached, this has increased to 11 feet and at Bahía San Luis Gonzales 14 foot spring tides may be experienced. Here at San Felipe the tides crest at 20 feet, finally surpassing 30 feet at the mouth of the Colorado.

These high tides, coupled with the shallow beach at San Felipe, results in the water line moving a half mile in and out with the flow of the tide. Breakers are not common in the upper gulf, but wind-driven waves may occur that are even rougher than the Pacific surf. It is possible to put out to sea on a mirror smooth surface, then to have to fight ones way back over a high-running sea, a few hours later.

Just to the north of the village is a small rock point with a small shrine erected on its summit. A well-worn trail leads up to this shrine, which supplies an excellent view of the village and the open sea. Hundreds of partially burned votary candles clearly indicate the respect the native fishermen have for the often innocent appearing Sea of Cortez.

To drive south of San Felipe a tourist card is required. This is a fairly safe graded dirt road as far south as Puertecitos. About three miles south of the village, a poor dirt road branches left, leading to Punta Diggs, Playa Estrella and Colonia Guiterrez, isolated Gulf Beaches, then returns to the main road about twenty miles farther south. These are pleasant and uncrowded places to camp in the early spring and late fall.

The main road wanders on southward, keeping a little ways inland, and is usually in fair condition most of the way. However in times of flash floods, such arroyo crossings as Arroyo El Moaomí may be impassable for a week after a bad storm. On the other hand, just north of Puertecitos, is located a short stretch of 'blow-sand' that can prove difficult after a hot dry wind-storm.

Puertecitos is a more or less primitive fishing resort. One may obtain gasoline, boats, launching service, limited supplies, basic cabins and some meals. Nearby is located an unusual phenomenon – a series of hot springs located just below the high tide line – so that one can alternate between dips in a hot spring and ocean bathing.

Below Puertecitos, the typical Baja California roadway begins. Even if you have made it to here in a conventional passenger car, from now on, a more rugged vehicle should be employed. Perhaps you can make it to Bahía San Luis Gonzaga, but remember, if you get into trouble, one cannot phone the Auto Club for help, or in fact, any other garage. The nearest help must come from San Felipe, perhaps up to a hundred rough miles away.

Recently (1968), with the increased interest on the part of the authorities, a road-grader has worked quite a ways south of here. But the basic road bed is still native soil, which may consist of loose sand, deep dust or rough rocks – so proceed with all possible caution. Just out of the resort are three sharp grades, of which the high one, Cuesta La Virgen, is rather difficult to surmount.

The road returns to the coast line, weaving in and out, until thirty miles below Puertecitos, one comes on an attractive intimate cove, Oakies Landing. So far, one may obtain camping sites and rent boats to explore and fish the nearby islands. But it seems likely that in the near future, other facilities will become available.

Another seventeen miles brings one to the beautiful Bahía San Luis Gonzaga, once the supply port for Misíon Santa María. (Here is as good a point as any to start a search for the legendary 'lost Misíon Santa Isabel' with its hidden pearls and gold) Long a roadside stop, it is beginning to develop into quite a resort with such modern conveniences as an air strip, gasoline and cold cerveza.

This is as far as one should attempt to drive without all the equipment that is needed for the La Paz run. In fact, the next stretch from here to Laguna Chapala can prove to be one of the most difficult of any on the Trans-Peninsular trek.

Las Islas

THE ISLANDS of La Frontera are few in number, small and barren, most being hardly more than waterless rocks. None was inhabited by the native Indians, and now only two are manned by the military and lighthouse keepers, who rely on imported supplies, including their drinking water.

The largest group, Islas Los Coronados, which lie about six miles below the prolongation of the International Border, are clearly visible from San Diego, so much so that one hardly realizes that they are an outpost of a foreign nation. Located a scant seven miles off the mainland, they consist of four islands two of some size. The first, North Island, is about a mile in length and rises 467 feet above sea level. These islands are volcanic in nature and not extensions of mainland ridges. North Island is a popular fishing area, as the slopes plunge directly to deep water. In fact, most of the boats seen in its waters are sport fishing boats out of National City.

North Island is a haven for birds: gulls, pelicans, petrels and cormorants, as well as two species of land birds, song sparrows and rock wrens. These latter birds are permanent residents. Their nearest relatives live on San Clemente Island, a distance much too great for them to travel, so perhaps in the far distant past these islands were connected, or at least bridged by a series of now submerged islets. Other birds, such as terns and shearwaters, visit these islands, but do not seem to nest here.

North Island is an ideal nesting place for gulls and similar birds, who lay their eggs in a small depression of soft sand. The low scattered growth consists of vidrío (crystal iceplant), daisies and sea dahlias, chollas, and other cactus. Probably one reason that the nesting birds chose this island is that there are no snakes nor predatory animals.

The two middle islands are really nothing but barren rocks, and they seldom see a human visitor.

South Island is almost two miles long, and its southern end reaches a height of 672 feet. Years ago an attempt was made to operate a resort hotel, but it proved unsuccessful. Its buildings now house a detachment of the Mexican Army. A lighthouse is

CHARTER BOAT APPROACHING LOS CORONADOS
PHOTO BY HELEN ELLSBERG

located on the southern tip of the island, and another light is shown from Puerto Cueva, a protected cove on the northeastern side that offers protection to stranded fishermen. South Island is well populated with rattlesnakes — hence no nesting birds.

The harbor of Ensenada, Bahía Todos Santos, is rather well sheltered. Punta San Miguel shields the northern side, while Punta Banda and its extending line of rocks offer shelter from southwest storms. Across the mouth are the two Todos Santos islands, low and barren. A powerful light is located on the northern, lower island. Years ago, inaccurate reporting by a writing gal gave birth to a legend that Robert Louis Stevenson had spent some time here and that these islands were the inspiration of his famous tale, 'Treasure Island'. Despite the fact that Stevenson was never south of Monterey, California, the rumor still persists, and you may be offered postal cards with a view of the islands and this misinformation.

From the plains of San Quintin, five remarkable volcanic cones arise, running in a line along the west side. The highest of these forms an island some three miles offshore. San Martín Island is about a mile in diameter, and crests in two summits. The southern one, 497 feet high, bears a forty foot deep crater, about the size of a football field. On the southeastern side of the island is a small circular lagoon, open to the sea at half tide. Here many birds and seals may be found.

Still farther south, about nine miles below Punta Baja and five miles offshore is San Geronimo Island. Basically, it is a barren rock, covered in many places with sand and whitened with guano. This mile long rock rises to a height of but 130 feet, and bears a light on its summit. The surrounding seas are filled with kelp beds, accented with outlying rocks.

On the Gulf side, islands are even scarcer off the shores of La Frontera. In the mouth of the Río Colorado are two, Montague Island, six miles in length, and Gore Island, about two miles long. These low-lying masses are a mixture of sand bars and sand dunes, being more desert than marine in appearance. For centuries the Colorado River and the Gulf of California have been waging a deadly battle to maintain their positions. But now that man has meddled by stripping the river of its sole weapon, the flood-carried sand and silt, by erecting a series of dams, it is now a matter of anxious speculation as to whether the Gulf may be able to extend its domain northward, perhaps again even recapturing the Imperial Valley.

References

Belden, L. Burr *Baja California Overland* third edition, La Siesta Press, Glendale, 1968. A collection of articles by an old Baja hand, updated to include descriptions of Mexico's 1968 new road-building.

Brenton, Thaddeus R. T., *Bahia* Westernlore Press, Los Angeles, 1961. Interesting chatty articles about a Norteamericano living in the city of Ensenada.

Brower, Kenneth, ed., *Baja California* Sierra Club, San Francisco, 1967. Handsome 'exhibit format' volume, beautifully illustrated, that fails to show any contact with or feeling for the people of Baja California.

Cannon, Ray. *The Sea of Cortez* Lane Book Co., Menlo Park, 1966. A fisherman-oriented book, colorful both in text and pictures.

Gerhard, Peter and Howard E. Gulick, *Lower California Guidebook* fourth edition, The Arthur H. Clark Co., Glendale, 1967. Still the standard log and guide to all of Baja California; accurate and detailed.

Goings, Robert A., *Guide to Baja California del Norte* Automobile Club of Southern California, Los Angeles, 1968. Completely new guide to La Frontera, but limited to main roads and 'main' side roads.

Jordon, Fernando, *El Otro Mexico* Electocopia, S. A., Mexico, D. F., 1967. Reprint edition authorized by the State of Baja California. Just possibly the best book yet to be written on Baja; unfortunately, it is only available in Spanish-language text.

Martinez, Pablo L., *A History of Lower California* Editorial Baja California, Mexico, D. F., 1960. The standard history, but poorly organized and contains numerous inaccuracies.

Meigs, Peveril, *The Dominican Mission Frontier of Lower California* University of California, Berkeley, 1935. The definitive study on the geography of La Frontera. Long out of print; rumored to be reprinted in 1968.

Robinson, John W., *Camping and Climbing in Baja* La Siesta Press, Glendale, 1967. A detailed guide to the Sierra Juárez and Sierra San Pedro Martír. Contains information on plants, animals, geology, etc.

Woods, Eugene, *How to Retire in Mexico on $2.47 a Day* Southwest Press, San Diego, 1965. Despite its how-to-do-it title, contains excellent information, much of it on Baja California. Details of the beach area not available in other books.

Index

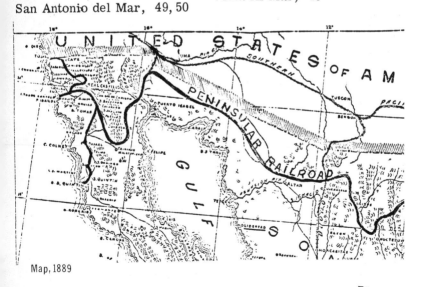

Map, 1889

La Siesta Press